KINGFISHER READERS

level 3

W9-CIH-707

Vikings

Philip Steele

KINGFISHER
NEW YORK

KINGFISHER
LONDON & NEW YORK

Copyright © Kingfisher 2014
Published in the United States by Kingfisher,
175 Fifth Ave., New York, NY 10010
Kingfisher is an imprint of Macmillan Children's Books, London.
All rights reserved.

Distributed in the U.S. and Canada by Macmillan,
175 Fifth Ave., New York, NY 10010

Library of Congress Cataloging-in-Publication data
has been applied for.

Series editor: Thea Feldman
Literacy consultant: Ellie Costa, Bank Street School for Children, New York

ISBN: 978-0-7534-7148-7 (HB)
ISBN: 978-0-7534-7149-4 (PB)

Kingfisher books are available for special promotions
and premiums. For details contact: Special Markets
Department, Macmillan, 175 Fifth Ave., New York, NY 10010.

For more information, please visit
www.kingfisherbooks.com

Printed in China
9 8 7 6 5 4 3 2 1
1TR/0314/WKT/UG/105MA

Picture credits
The Publisher would like to thank the following for permission to reproduce their material. Every care has been taken to trace copyright holders. However, if there have been unintentional omissions or failure to trace copyright holders, we apologize and will, if informed, endeavor to make corrections in any future edition.
Top = t; Bottom = b; Center = c; Left = l; Right = r
Cover Kingfisher; Pages 7 Peter Kuiper/Wikipedia;
9t Corbis/Werner Forman Archive; 9b Shutterstock/Kristina Postnikova; 12 Shutterstock/Mircea Bezergheanu; 15t Art Archive/ Oldsaksammlung, Oslo/Dagli Orti; 15b Corbis/Werner Forman Archive; 17 Corbis/Werner Forman Archive; 19 Corbis/Werner Forman Archive; 20 Alamy/Troy GB Images; 23 Corbis/Ted Spiegel; 26 Corbis/Ted Spiegel; 28 Art Archive/ Musee de la Tapisserie/Gianni Dagli Orti; all other illustrations from the Kingfisher archive.

Contents

Who were the Vikings?	4
Vikings at sea and home	6
Gods and giants	8
In the longhouse	10
Farming and food	12
Making beautiful things	14
Towns and trade	16
Off to war	18
Warriors and weapons	20
Raiders and settlers	22
Sailing west	24
Burials and burnings	26
The end of an age	28
Glossary	30
Index	32

Who were the Vikings?

Norway, Sweden, and Denmark are countries in the north of Europe. The lands there have lakes, mountains, big forests, and rocky coasts. The winters are cold and snowy, but the summers are warm.

The people who lived on these lands between 750 and 1100 CE are known as Vikings. The name Viking means "sea **raider**." Vikings traveled the seas and attacked other people. But they were also farmers, fishermen, and **traders**.

There are many stories called sagas written about Vikings. They tell us how Vikings lived long ago.

Viking tales
At Viking gatherings, poets called skalds told exciting tales about battles, ships, treasures, and monsters.

Vikings at sea and home

Vikings traveled far and wide. They raided towns and villages. They seized gold from churches, burned buildings, and stole cattle. They killed people or carried them off to become slaves.

Vikings were not just raiders. They also cleared forests, built towns, farmed the land, and fished.

There were many successful Viking traders, as well as expert craft workers. Viking settlers passed laws too.

Viking writing

The Vikings spoke a language we call Old Norse. It was sometimes written down in letters called runes. You can see runes on this stone.

Gods and giants

Vikings believed in many gods. Odin was the father of the gods. People believed that he rode an eight-legged horse. On stormy nights, they thought they could see Odin galloping across the sky. Odin had two pet **ravens**. They flew around the world every day and told him what they saw.

God of thunder
This is a carving of Thor, who was the god of thunder and lightning. He had a big hammer, which he used to fight giants and monsters.

'ikings believed in other worlds too, 'here there were giants, monsters, snakes, nd spirits. At the center of the **universe** 'as a gigantic ash tree, named Yggdrasil say IG-druh-sil).

The way to the gods
Vikings believed that the world of humans was connected to the world of the gods by a great rainbow bridge.

In the longhouse

Many Vikings lived in farming **settlement** with stables and barns. The biggest building was the longhouse. It was a long wooden hut with a **thatched** roof.

Inside, it was dark and smoky. A fire burne for warmth, and the floor was covered in dried grass. Raised platforms along the walls were used as beds or seats. Families, farm workers, and slaves all slept here.

Vomen prepared
ood and wove
loth on a loom.
Men repaired
shing lines, tools,
nd weapons.

Games and dice
On winter nights, Vikings sat by the fire and played dice or board games such as chess.

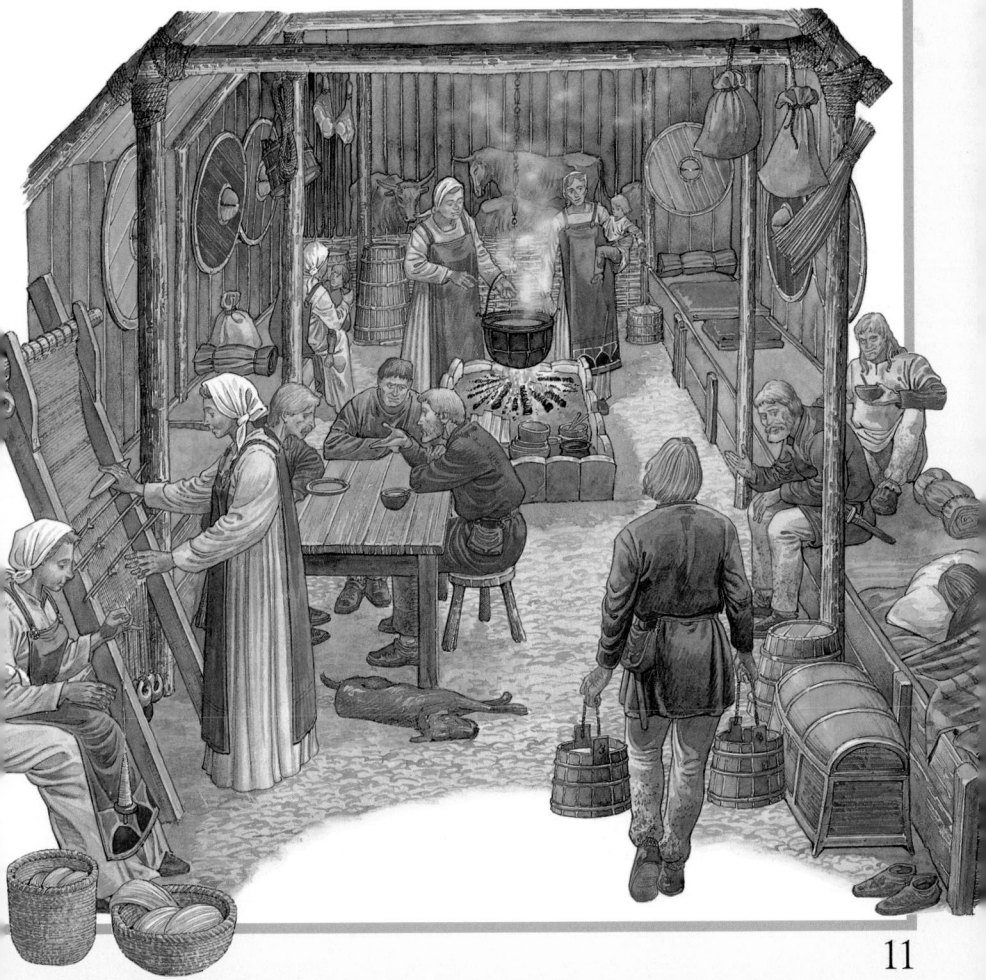

Farming and food

Viking farmers grew wheat, barley, rye, peas, and cabbages. They raised geese, sheep, goats, pigs, horses, and cattle. They got eggs, milk, meat, wool, and leather from the animals.

The Vikings also hunted wild birds, reindeer, and wild **boar**. The seas were full of fish, such as cod and herring, which they caught in nets.

Farmers raised goats for meat and milk.

Drinking horns
The Vikings drank wine, beer, or mead from hollow cattle horns. Mead was a strong drink made from honey.

eople often salted or dried meat and fish
o it would keep longer. They cooked over a
re or stewed food in **cauldrons**.

Making beautiful things

Viking women wove thread into cloth to make clothes and blankets. They wore simple, long dresses with long **tunics** over them. The shoulder straps were fastened with beautiful pins and chains. Me wore long **breeches** anc woollen tunics.

Vikings made jewelry from gold, silver, anc colored stone.

iking craftsmen
rved horns,
alrus tusks,
ood, and stones.

This wood carving shows a Viking making a sword.

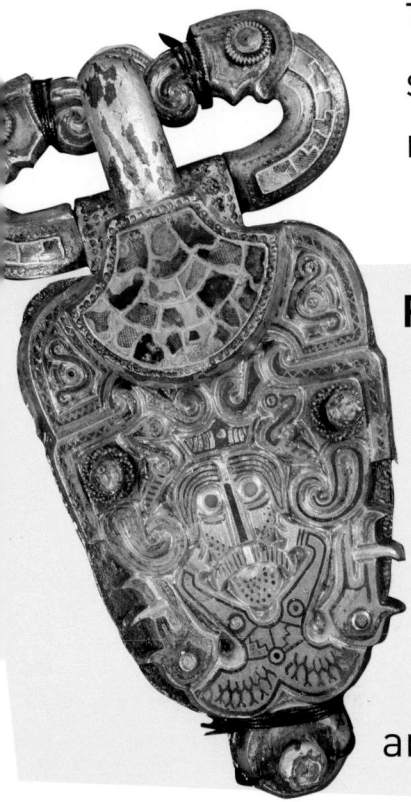

Pictures and patterns

Viking designs had swirling patterns and included birds, snakes, and monsters.

Towns and trade

Most towns were built by rivers or **harbors**, since most travel took place on the water. There were few good roads.

Houses and workshops were made of wood. People dug ditches or built fences around the towns to prevent enemy attacks.

eople bought
ood, tools,
ots and pans,
nd jewelry in
own markets.
ilks, furs, and
pices from
raway places
ere for
ale too.

Viking money

At first, Vikings did not have their own coins. So people just traded things at the market.

Off to war

Vikings built many types of boats. They had little rowing boats and sturdy ships that carried heavy **cargo**. Their finest ships, called **longships**, were used for crossing the oceans or going to war.

'iking longships were designed to be fast. ach ship was rowed by a crew of 30 or ıore men. Every man had one oar. 'he ship had a square sail made of ool or linen.

ll the sailors were also fighters, and they ere heavily armed. Shields were hung long the sides of the ship to protect the owers from enemy arrows.

Dragon ships
A longship had a high wooden **prow**. It was often carved into a snarling dragon shape.

Warriors and weapons

Most Vikings were farmers and fishermen who joined their **jarl** for raids.

They wore everyday clothes into battle, as well as a helme made of leather or iron.

A jarl often wore somethin called a mail shirt that was made from iron rings

ikings fought
ith iron swords,
pears, axes, and
ows and arrows.
heir big, round
nields were made
f wood, with
n iron knob in
ne middle.

Berserk!
Some warriors worked themselves into a fury before a battle. They were called "berserkir," and they wore shirts of bear skin. Today we still use the word "berserk" to mean crazy.

Raiders and settlers

Viking raiders wanted to be rich and powerful. They attacked villages, towns, and big cities. They attacked Great Britain, Ireland, Germany, France, and Spain.

The Vikings set up winter camps in foreign lands. Then they built new settlements overseas and took control of whole regions.

Archaeologists find Viking remains under the streets of Dublin, in Ireland.

'he Vikings
ook over York
n England.
n France,
ney took
ver a large
rea of
and called
Normandy.

Nicknames
Viking warriors had scary nicknames, such as Erik Bloodaxe and Thorfinn Skull-Splitter.

Sailing west

The Vikings sailed west across the oceans. Between 874 and 930 CE, they settled in Iceland. There were few trees, so they built longhouses from stone, grass, and earth. Wherever they settled, they set up **assemblie** to make laws and solve arguments.

Sometimes storms blew Viking longships even further west and the sailors sighted unknown lands.

Viking assemblies were held in the open air.

Viking settlers hunted walrus and seals off the icy coasts of Greenland.

n 982 CE, Erik the Red led settlers to an icy nd. He called it Greenland, hoping that his name would attract more people.

rik's son was Leif the Lucky. In about 002 CE, he sailed down the coast of orthern North America. The Vikings tried to settle in North America, but they were fiercely attacked by the Native Americans.

Burials and burnings

Vikings returned from their travels with a lot of treasure. In times of war or trouble, they buried the treasure to keep it safe. People are still discovering these Viking treasures.

Viking treasure found in Sweden

In the hall of Odin
Vikings believed that warriors who died in battle met the god Odin. They feasted forever in his great hall, Valholl.

rchaeologists also find treasure
places where Vikings were buried.
ome dead Viking chiefs were put on their
ips, which were then set on fire. Others
ere placed inside ships and buried
eneath mounds of earth.

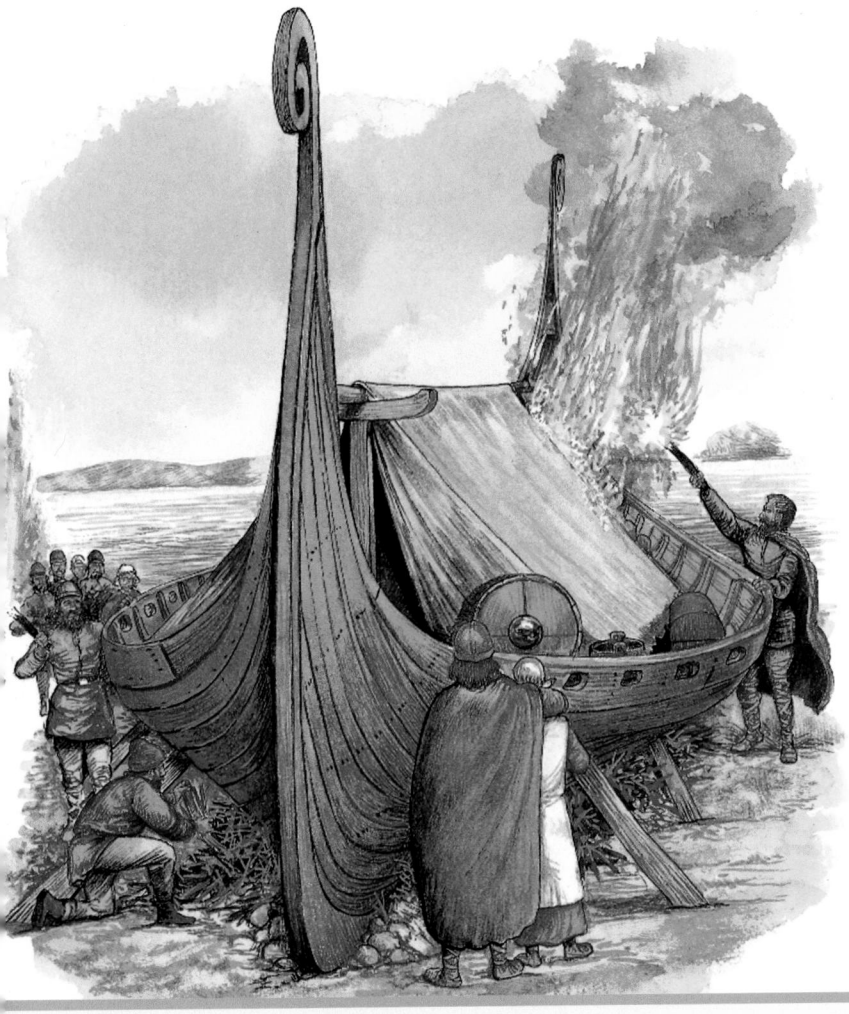

The end of an age

After about 960 CE, many Vikings became Christians. For years, people wore the hammer symbol of the god Thor alongside the cross of Christianity. By the 1080s, all the Viking lands were Christian. The Vikings became part of larger kingdoms, and they stopped raiding.

When the Normans invaded England in 1066 their boats looked just like Viking longships.

escendants of the Vikings who settled in
ance, called Normans, conquered large
rts of Europe, from England to Italy.
he old Viking lands make up the modern
untries of Denmark, Sweden, Norway,
d Iceland.

VIKING DATES

789 CE	Vikings start to raid the British Isles.
841	Vikings are based in Dublin, Ireland.
867	Vikings capture York, England.
874	Vikings settle Iceland.
911	Vikings win Normandy, in France.
960	Christianity starts in Viking lands.
982	Erik the Red reaches Greenland.
1002	Leif the Lucky explores northern North America.
c.1100	The Viking age comes to an end.

Glossary

archaeologist someone who digs up and studie ancient ruins and remains

assembly a group of people who make laws an important decisions

boar a wild pig

breeches a type of pants

cargo goods loaded on a ship

cauldron a big, metal cooking pot

descendant a relative of a person who lived a long time ago

harbor a place where ships stay and are prepared for their journeys

jarl a Viking chief or nobleman

longship a long, narrow ship with oars and a single sail

prow the front of a ship

ider someone who attacks others and steals
om them

ven a big, black bird in the crow family

ttlements an area where people build places
live and work that had no such places before

atched covered with straw or reeds

ader a person who buys and sells goods

nic a long, loose garment that is usually worn
er other clothing

aiverse everything that exists, including
ater space

Index

animals 8, 12, 25
assemblies 24

clothing 14, 20, 21

Erik the Red 25

farmers 5, 7, 12, 20
food 11, 12, 13, 17

gods 8–9, 26, 28

jarls 20
jewelry 15, 17

Leif the Lucky 25
longhouses 10, 24
longships 18, 19, 24, 27, 28

markets 16, 17
money 17

raids 5, 6, 7, 20, 22
runes 7

sagas 5
settlers 7, 22, 24, 25
slaves 6, 10

traders 17
treasure 5, 26, 27

warriors 20–21, 23